First, Love.

© 2021. *First, Love* by Monique Lyttle.

Work Cited: KJV & NIV bible

Published by: Monique Lyttle

Text Design by: Monique Lyttle

Cover Design by: Tarik Lewis

Illustrations: Marley Berot

ISBN: 978-0-578-91476-3

First, Love.

MONIQUE LYTTLE

what I have written in this little book are short stories,
written as poetry and handwritten letters,
expressing the emotions from my own life's journy'ws.

beginning from the day I finally wanted better,
and was actually willing to go through the terrains
to get better.

understanding not everything I believed was actually true,
and not everything true is out to hurt me.

my hope is for us all to know we are not alone,
and for us to have hope in the Christ of God.
He is the very essence of LOVE.

GOD IS LOVE!

before i begin,
i want to send a shout out to literally ~everyone~!

thank you all so much!
thank you for loving me.
thank you for trying to love me.
thank you for the hurt.
thank you for the accountability.
and most of all,
thank you for the support.

here's to healing wounds...

effectively.

january 18, 2018

i think my issue is,
while trying to love everyone else,
i forgot about loving myself.
and every time i feel anger towards someone
or something,
it is a reflection
of what i already dislike in myself.
since i naturally
and subconsciously
know the things i dislike within myself,
i can easily pick it out within other people.
therefore, creating a cycle of
anger
rejection
and inner confusion
rarely understood by the common human being
who is also suffering
in their own anger.

and i get it.
this is why
it's important
to find the root of our anger,
understand it
and embrace the understanding
with the original reason
of why we put ourselves in that position
at all times.

the thing is,
though,
this dangerous ditch
we dare to enter
in hopes
to open our own hearts
to our own selves,
can either defeat us

or make us stronger.

january 18, 2018

right now,

i can feel myself
constantly digging
through my own sinking sand.
metaphorically,
obviously,
because in this case,

i know i'm going to make it.

but it's hard.
it's so freaking hard
and i cannot fathom
the practice it will take
to get to the space i need to be.
because, i am constantly breaking
myself apart
and rebuilding,
and i am
worn.

part of me wants to say
it's because i'm bad at this,
and i would fight
defending those words,
but this just shows
how much more work needs to be done.

january 18, 2018

i am my own art piece.
a gift from God.
and i have the choice
to clean off all the gunk
that made its way
to
in
and around
this art i call my soul.

i try to tell myself this everyday,
and it is so hard, i tell you.

but
with no further adieu,
i will say to you
that without understanding
we will move blindly.
slow and steady wins the race.
and trust all that is controlled
and uncontrollable
with God.

this is merely my beginning piece.

my preface.
my debut.
i am
the jack of all trades,
aad i can do all things through Christ,
who strengthens me.

love is patient.
love is kind.
it does not envy,
it does not boast,
it is not easily angered.
it keeps no record of wrongs.
love does not delight in evil
but rejoices with the truth.
it always protects,
always trusts,
always hopes,
always perseveres.

love, literally, never fails.

1 corinthians 13:4-8

contents

The Beginning of my last.

here's to letting go, and realizing I am not my own.

keep it.
i no longer want it.
you've already hurt me enough.
i want nothing from you.
i can't trust
anything you present to me
anymore.

they say,
real recognizes real,
so what does that mean for me
if everything you present to me,
i view as a snake in disguise?

i hate...
don't like, i mean...
i don't like snakes.
i want to,
but i don't.

i want to be vulnerable,
yet i close up...
every time you are around.
but i am trying
to be open
to feeling.

bite me...
so i know it's real.

my love!
catch my drift!
i'm just...
just, just
trying to be better.

you remind me of a woman
who has no idea
how wonderful she is.

a woman full
of so much love.
but i can tell
you're addicted to pain.

you say
ow and *'never again,'*
but i can tell
you would stick your foot
in a snakes mouth
just to see how it feels.

why, babe?
i love you,
i care.

stop numbing.
feel what you should.

i see his soul.
i see his heart.
i want to help nurture it
for the sake of being
a wife.

i say all of this,
but when will i stop being in denial?
why is this so difficult?
why is love, love?
i'm not even fully there yet,
but...

no one ever talks about
how it feels to fall in love.
are we actually falling,
or are we just standing
trying our best
to get used to the comfort?
discomfort, i mean.
falling probably gives us
the butterflies,
like we're... on a swing.

what are these?
are these nerves?
my body is hot.
this man can warm my heart
and boil my blood.

yo!
am i really in love?
ya, obviously...
but, really?
why is this so
hard to accept, even?
this is so weird!
instead of falling,
i want to find another way to do this.

i should just sit down.
maybe lie down.
lay low.
spend time with love
and everything it offers.
pay attention.
be here,
be now.
but the problem is,
i am scared of being rejected.
i need to stop being scared.
look at what i'm causing myself...

rejection.

i just want to learn, man.
i want to learn about the stars.
i want to learn more about God.
i want to learn multiple languages,
but i also want to learn about you.
i love knowledge, i want to know every thing.
but, i also want to know you.
i want to learn about God with you.
i want to love God with you.
i want to love you,
through Him.

we don't get everything we want,
though, do we?
or what we think we want.
think about this.
what's the difference between
what we want
and what we already have?
what's for you,
will always be for you, they say.
what's not...
well, then...
it's just not.
especially when it's not what God wants.

"take delight in the Lord,
and He will give you the desires of your heart."

the heart doesn't lie.

you are like a stepping stone...
the one i take towards
my own self-love.
i've seen the steps
countless times, but
now, i am noticing
the distinction of my soul
and the intricate design
of my heart.

the heart is deceitful above all things.
and desperately wicked. who can know it?

i met Someone lately,
who is not so new.
i heard a lot about Him before
about all that He can do.
all that He knows,
which is... it's everything.
He knows everything.
and He's so patient.
and so kind.
so loving.
He holds nothing against me.
He is like the man of my dreams
except he's much bigger
than your basic man.
He?
embodies love like no other.
no longer do i have to sleep
feeling cold and lonely.
misunderstood.
no longer do i have to look
for something to ease my soul
or hold on to my own life.

My grace is sufficient for you,

He said.
He's right,
i feel whole.

come to Me,
all of you that labor,
and are heavy laden
and I will give you rest.
for My yoke is easy,
and My burden is light.

for those who really saw me,
knew i never wanted to feel anything.

a blank blob.
that is what i thought i desired.
yet i have received a peace
surpassesing all understanding
for the first time in my life.

i can see Love
i can feel Love
i can choose Love

and greater LOVE
has no man than this
that a man would
lay down His life
for His friends.

He called me His friend.
He is so protective.
i want to go wherever He goes.
which means, i will leave
everything i own
to be with Him.
call me "crazy,"
but, that's LOVE!
GOD IS LOVE.
and He gave me
a new heart
to love Him with.

i am not afraid

sometimes,
it hurts.
it hurts to love.
it hurts to be here
and now...
it even hurts to gain wisdom
for how else will we learn?
those who dont listen
must feel.
that hurt.
it hurts to stay humble.
it hurts to embrace
everything you feared once before.

it hurts to move forward.
it hurts to be
the person you need to be
for someone else.
it hurts to turn away.
and for someone
who had been addicted to pain...
it is to my surprise
how much i think of running away
from all the good things in life.

some twisted story this is
for me to want better,
but be afraid of getting better.

of being better.

of being me.

the fear of the unexpected
must go.

now tell me this,
is it truly pain i'm feeling?

or
is it just
the uncomfortable feeling
of adjustment?
i know it is,
but to face myself means
no more looking back.

i fear.
that...
that is why i look back.
i fear
the future.
the rejection.
but
God has not given me
the spirit of fear.
He has given me the Spirit
of power and of love
and of a sound mind.
so maybe i don't really fear.
that is not
what is happening here.
it's because i want to fear.

fear is where
my comfort lies.

fear is my excuse
to continue being the same...

same friends,
same coping mechanisms,
same anger,
same awkwardness,
same victim.

i am not a victim.
i am not awkward.
i do not have anger issues.
i no longer have to deal
with my detrimental coping mechanisms.
i,
am not afraid of growing
in a different direction
than the people i have known for
years.
i am not afraid.

today,
i heard musicians
do things with their hands
that made the hearts in the room
go silent.
i heard voices
that made the hearts of the audience
sing along.
i saw God's work
at work.
i thought,
i don't think they know
how blessed they are.
this gift.
how it affects people.
but,
they do.
they know.
... they know.
so,
i continued thinking.
thinking on
the thought of being wrong
about them.
it's me.

it's me.
i am the one
who does not know
how blessed i am.
my gift.
how it affects people.
you remind me of a woman
who does not know how wonderful she is.
my words.
come to realize,
i have never really took the time
to really appreciate
what God did
in me.
what is it
that makes me so blind
to myself?

heaven on earth

the place i want to be
before my Father returns.
i want to run away, though.
up into the heavens.
i wanna be home.

i wanna be home, home.
so,
we can say
not much has changed.
not in that area.
i've been looking for
an escape
since i first knew
how unbearable pain can be.
the anger
the fear...
remove me from this earth,
i would ask.
yet here i am
19 years later,
still learning
i am here for a reason.
God still has huge plans for me.
plans for me to prosper,
and not harm me.
plans to give me hope
and a future.

this...
this should be a fulfilling word,
but what is it
that is holding me back?
what am i not letting go of
so that i may live deeply
in my heaven on earth?
what have i not accepted?
what have i not come to peace with?
what am i doing?
change my view,
oh Lord.
i can take this,
but i can't.
not anymore.
bring me the peace of mind i need
and the perspective change i need
to increase the joy
You have given me to continue on.
i am Yours.

what is this?

a hot flash?

i keep looking back.

on the files

that still have yet to be gone away.

touches that made me cringe...

no.

why didn't he listen to me?

why won't anyone listen to me?

my past,

coming into the now...

someone,

please bring it back down.

Lord,

take this cup away from me.

the things you may not know

you don't know what it's like
to sit so close to you.
how it is to be so ever aware
of the slightest touch.
i look at you
in your eyes...
a little delicacy,
i would call that.
to see your truest self
you do not know
the happiness it brings me.

you don't know
the measure it takes
to keep myself apart from you.
how much i limit my hugs for you.
fighting myself
to be your friend...
you don't know what it's like
to choose the better part
of our relationship.
i chose to grow in love
with you.
just grow.
whatever the outcome.
i desired to be with you,
but as the same flowers
growing from the same dirt.
we grow together,
as life brings us up.
different experiences,
but same darkness.
same fight.
same love.
same light.

i miss the days
when things were so platonic
between us.
the days i felt nothing.
the days i didn't care.
the days i wasn't so self conscious.
i don't want to go back,
but i want to be here.
not to rely on you
as a friend,
but to have a friendship
that is pure
and real.
i think i failed you
sometimes.
as a friend.
the way i used you.
the way i blamed you.
the way i fell in love with you.
or thought i did.
the way i let it affect us.
i don't want to be like everyone else.
i just wanted to be there for you.
because i knew your pain.
because,
even though you used me, too
you still were there for me
in ways no other person had been.
i finally see why God chose you.
why it was my life
you were put in.
for all things work for the good
of those who love God.
even this.
even now.
this thing i used to hate.
this love.
going from the "feelings"
i swept under the rug,
to making a choice.
this process.
this thorn in my flesh.
teaching me how to love,
i thank God for you.

look at me.

i am God's child.
i am not an alcoholic.
i am not a liar.
i am not fake.
i am not broken.
i am not a failure.
i am not lost.
i am not what has happened to me.
i am not what i have done.
i am not who people say i am.
i am not even who i think i am.
i am not the mistakes i make.

even to this day,
i am not my pain.

[PAGE30]

uncertainty

i don't even know what my heart desires
but i know You're going to give it to me.
i can trust and expect that
because i believe You.
i can wait,
because You teach me patience.
You are Faithfulness,
and so i trust You.
in every,
why me?
will i put my trust in You.
every stress,
my trust
will be still
in You.
in every cry,
will i know
You are right here
with me.
willing to hold my hand
and lift me up.
my Helper
my Provider
Jehovah Jireh.

dear Daddy,

the wind blows
and i do trust it's Yours.
i stand on two feet
and i trust
it's You who is responsible
for holding me up,
or holding me down
as they'd say... You know.

the Foundation is solid.
whether water or stone;
never holding me back,
i can trust You got me.
i'm walking...
i'm moving...
even when i have fallen
You never leave me alone
You teach me to crawl first,
never being ashamed
of looking less than
how You see me
teaching me
to limp into my healing.

why does she walk like that?
why does she talk like that?
why have things changed?

eyes on You,
i block them out.
love is love.
YOU, God, are Love.
thank you.

sincerely,
Your daughter

[PAGE32]

love.
a best friend.
beauty beyond knowledge.
a reason to smile.
even during the most hurtful times.
friendship
growth
to feel so close,
yet so far,
we become stronger.
one laugh
reminding me
of our good,
our amazing,
our most trusting,
relationship.
big ole sap
i would be for you.
i could cry at the thought
of everything
between you and i...
great and small.
your voice,
your laugh.
my heart sings.
a best friend.
one undeserving.
one love.
one understanding.
thank you,

happy birthday.

ditch.
been digging myself out
or, well...
that was the plan
to do everything myself.
make my own life
live by it
my own world...
everyone must go
where they fit
leave if you must.
maybe i would rather it that way.
i would rather a lot of things
like if you knew the real me
without my effort
to reveal it to you.
i would rather me to feel free
to be myself
around you.
around anyone for that matter.
i wish the negatives wouldn't pull so hard
on my positives
to get me to think a certain way.
so i could sink, but
i refuse to go deeper
than where i've gone.
the more i dig myself out
the more holes i find
giving me the heebie jeebies.
i just can't do this on my own
anymore.
tell me,
which is worse?
being all alone
or feeling like you're all alone?
Yahshua, get me out of this.
this way of thinking,
being...
grab my hands, please.
before i find a new hole.

rejection.
also known as
my God's protection.
when the words,
i don't want you.
from another man
translates to -
you don't want him,
from my Father.
especially not right now.
when not getting the job
i thought i wanted
really means i wouldn't thrive
to my greatest capacity.

with everything i thought i wanted...

rejection is nothing
compared to what is really for me.

it's a reunion

my memories don't serve me right.
i see smiles and laughter
clear as day
but it's as though
the details of my life
have been erased...
yet
no harm done.

sometimes,
i worry my memories
will prove its failure.
the fear of conversations
with old friends come up and...
i think, *what if...*
what if they're offended?
when we talk about the old times,
and... nothing comes to mind.
what if they still see me as the old me?
special, yes. but, mean.
i was malicious.
i think i'm thinking too much.

i remember the time
i put glue all over his lunchbox.
did he know that was me?
the name i called him...?
as we talk, anyhow,
i gain another meaning
of what it is to be free.
to let go
despite inevitable judgment.
i don't know him anymore,
yet it's as though he never left.
smiles and laughter.
i can't tell if he's just normal,
or weird enough to continue a conversation.
with me, that is.
not sure how he found me,
but i'm glad he did.
i can thank God for that.

the sound of the music
tells me everything is okay.
this peace...
this pure peace
is a beautiful symphony.
there's no getting lost
in the music.
i'm prepared.
prepared for every single change in tone.
i'm prepared.
prepared to face it all.
head on.
no weight on my shoulders.
i walk in peace.
look at my shoes.
all comfort.
let me not grow weary.

i'm not weary.
not when i wait.
not when i'm open to listen.
so i incline my ears...
i'm ready.

speak, Lord.
Your servant is listening.

maybe i should write
with no goal of being artistic.
i'd like to say how i feel.
i'd like to be beauty without trying
internally, that is.
that's funny.
i just finished working on my face.
exfoliating, moisturizing... aiming to be
bright.
i'm trying.
i want to talk.
i want to talk it all out.
for me.
for you.
for us...
for them.
i want to be.
be the woman God has made me to be.
i'm not lonely, i'm not alone.
i feel lonely, but i'm not alone.
issues come up,
and i can see i'm not rooted in Life.
not deeply anyway.
it's a weird feeling....
to be so close, yet so far.
is it my fault,
or is it my appointed timing?
not lost,
but i'm curious.

and the ton overwhelms me.
the ton of responsibilities i see around me.
He takes the burden,
but what must i do to let go?
is there more to it?
my eyes burn and i see sadness
trying to make its way over.
no, i'm just tired.
leave me alone.
not here to sulk,
i just want to live in excellence.
hard work.
hard work.
am i capable?
i like to believe i am,
but i have my doubts.
shut it up.
those doubts.
speaking depression over my life,
i no longer want parts.
the hardest work isn't too hard at all.
what's hard is choosing to take the dive.
choosing to continue.
sounds like love.

toe dips is how i take on responsibility
i want to be pushed in,
but to be willing to jump in myself,
knowing of the cloud that awaits to hold me up
holds a different level of motivation.
God will help me jump.

God helps me jump.
and the cloud seems to soften
more and more
after each landing.
let me lay.

write me a letter
and tell me everything i shouldn't know.
everything you think

i shouldn't know, i mean.
i think i deserve to know
everything.
be honest with me.
you could look at my heart,
but don't touch.
tell me what you think.
i need my eyes open to myself
let me see what i'm not seeing.
show me yourself.
tell me what you think
about us.
are we good?
are we growing?
have i hurt you?
are you well?
i can tell you're interested
but i'm not sure you're all there.
say something.

okay,
you've never hurt me before.
we've known each other for so long
and maybe i don't remember
the things you've said to me,
but this.....
i wasn't expecting this.
i don't want to think
you did this to hurt me.
perhaps i'd be lying to myself.
trying to put blame somewhere
it shouldn't be.

none of this even is about me,
but why couldn't i have been consid-
ered?

perhaps i was.
perhaps all of this
could have been avoided.
perhaps it shouldn't even matter to
me.
perhaps i forgive you.
perhaps i understand.
perhaps i just don't want to feel
this way anymore.
perhaps we should just move forward.

how could this be?
i'm hurt
and i would not have thought
you would do this to me.
but
this really isn't even about me,
is it?
your mistakes
are not revenge.
thoughts come up
and i think it's my Father
seeking to avenge.
we reap what we sew, don't we?
so maybe i did something
to deserve this.
looking for blame,
i find confusion.
ignorance may be bliss,
but not this one.

fusing possible explanations,
i tell my mind to keep quiet
and focus.
i feel bogus just thinking
sometimes...
asking when it'll be over.
free me from this.
my enemy has me tied
in certain areas of my mind,
i could scream.
i could scream,
but i don't.
i could scream,
but i won't...
how would it be
to acknowledge the anguish
i think i feel.
is it even real?

be still
and keep your eyes on Me.
slow down,
and walk with Me.
talk with Me.
lean on Me.
choose Me.
in all your thoughts,
choose Me.
pick Me.
love Me.

sounds like Someone's at the door.

i speak less
in order to hear more.

i'd like to have dinner with you, i'll cook,
He says.

come in.
my hunger is deep,
and i need meat.
heart, soul, and mind
i need to eat.
teach me how to be
and feed me as i go.
i need more peace,
will You cook that for me, too, please?
my own food is not enough.
plus, i'd rather it not be this tough.

dear future husband,

i'm not positive
i know who you are.
neither am i sure,
if i know who i am.
or if i'll be ready
for you.
but i trust God
when it comes to you.
my heart is God's heart
and i pray yours is in His hands, too.
i want to please God
when i please you.
and i can only hope
to be treated like i'm God's child, too.
that's right.
we are God's children before anything,
and we will be treated as such.

i pray,
in Jesus' name,
for all giants to be crushed.
we stand on their necks...
it's a family sport.
rabid dogs on a leash,
we remain untouched.
and i pray we never pet them,
but if we do,
repentance is a must.
keeping each other accountable,
i pray for honesty
alright, and now i gotta pee.
excuse me,
take me as i am
and God will make me who i am
supposed to be.

thank you for listening to me.

love,
monique

perfection.
it's my biggest problem.
wondering why
i'm so hard on myself...
fighting to get out of this section,
i feel bad.
disheartened.
he keeps reminding me
all i do is screw up.
he says i'm the worst,
for feeling....
suggesting i could have done better.
i'm useless, he says.
what do i do
to get him out of my head?

write it down.

the words in my heart...
i can't tell if they're all pure.
i feel pain in its realest form.
necessary,
yet i feel drawn.
drawn away from something.
drawn into something.
drawn out of everything.
the fight to feel included
but to know
i'm called to live excluded
my heart hurts,
so i feel intruded.
rugged splinters in my flesh
struggling to still choose to do my best.
it hurts to touch
better yet,
it hurts to snatch it out.
and i pout at my uncertainty
feeling stupid as can be.
from clogged wounds i chose to ignore
to inevitable bleeding...
i'd be so sore,
but then i get my healing.
finally, i'll have a clean house.
jump off a building
land on a cloud.

feelings are fleeting,
but i know my heart
is still beating.
plus, no longer
am i bleeding
on everyone i thought i loved.
what a mess i made
furthest from the One above.
not a maid service,
but He cleanses me everyday.
and it's not may,
but even when i don't know it,
His reign still has me growing.

let's be kind
to our own selves.

as i minded others' business,
it's the truth when i say
i forgot about myself.
i ran out of hands
before i could even lend myself help.
held hostage
where they take me for granted.
blindfolded for so long,
i can hear their voices
clearer than the day we landed.
big red flag
posted across my eyes.
how could i have missed it?
no balance in the scales,
i wonder who tipped it.

let's talk waste.
because that is what i'm doing.
with this bag, that is.
but i hope i don't waste my love..
is that even a thing?
i could waste my time,
i could waste my energy...
my life...
but what about my love?
my peace, yes,
i know.
but what is love
that it can be wasted?
if love lasts forever,
can i run out of it?
if i jump into another pool,
does love come with me?
will love come with me?
will love follow me wherever i go?
does love know me?
can love hide from me?
will fear push my love away?
should i hold on tight,
or will love always be there?
if i live in love,
but i question it,
what does it mean?
what does it mean
if i tempt hate
after not finding love
where i thought it would be?
can love claim me,
and not really be there?
is there a facade?
do they know?
do they know?
so many questions
i already have the answers to,
but i ask because i'm not sure what to do.
and that's when i lie to myself,
knowing to stand firm
in Truth,
in Love,
and in my own vulnerability.
moving forward
things break off,
and my arms feel lighter?
... do they?

close the doors.

you know what...
let's get straight to the point.
i am sick and tired
of seeing her.
what a fan of boys to men she was,
and i'm not talking about the singing group.
i'm talking about the young men.
those grown boys whose age differences
are not worth the greater pain.
i'm sick and tired of seeing her
choose not to feel.
seeing her choose
not to feel good enough.
sick and tired of watching her
think she's not good enough
for anyone.
she has been abused and left.
left to figure things out.
left to figure what that meant.
every touch,
and why every single one of them
told her to be quiet.
i watched her learn, too.
i watched her be influenced
by manipulation.
i watched her be influenced by loneliness.
i even watched her
as the women on television taught her
how to give away everything
that'll make her a woman.
i watched her do her own thing.
but that's just childhood, right?
her story doesn't end there.
not even where she forces her enjoyment
so her boyfriend could feel good.
her boyfriend.....
i heard her tell him no that day,
and he never listened.
no apology,
just, ha... *i feel like i raped you.*
i watched her stay silent.

what a pro, she became.

detachment makes *his* name known in her,
and isolation took over.
not a care in the world,
she has finally become
the one's who hurt her.
don't care. don't care.
still don't care, she said.
deep inside,
i know she does.
i hope she does.

[PAGE52]

can you blame her?
she did what she had to
to survive.
you'd think her anger kept her alive.
she made a bubble for herself
and sat all day to watch prey.

if anything,
i should be the one blamed.
i was the one who watched.
i watched it all happen.
even when it was done,
i hit the replay button.
i watched.

but scratch all that,
and let's count her blessings.
at the top of the list
without a doubt
is the Most High.
she has been made
more than a conqueror
and i'm pretty sure she can fly!
she's got His grace...
what a blessing it is
to even see His face.
looks like she's got His smile, too!
light seen within,
i see her!
she could fight!
reflecting the Christ of God,
she shines so bright.
out of nowhere,
i hear the devil
whispering into my ear,
don't forget
she's damaged goods.

excuse me,
have you seen
what God can do?
even with insignificance?
don't think i've forgotten about you.
He spat on the dirt, yes,
but He made a blind man see.
yea, she's still blessed.

[PAGE53]

let go,
said the Lamb
behind my mind.
it's time.

i wrote little notes...
putting them in balloons,
they float away
just like my thoughts.

let go,
i whisper to myself.
i wrote down every pain
and set them to burn
in the cooking pots.
let God.

i forgot
what it takes to forgive....
yes, it took me a lot.
slowly cooked out of my mind,
too gone to hear the knocks outside.
but it looks like i made it out
just in time.
i let go.
i chose.
my peace vs. my pain
my joy vs. being lame...
i made it out.

i become welcomed to a place
where love knows no boundaries.
even in my imperfection
does love find me.
love guides me in one direction
and love saves me.
putting me in a life boat
the life boat saves me
the wind blows where it wishes
and puts me in my place.
therefore, do i now live in love
right where my destiny lies.
and the Son shines on my face.
it's so hot, but i still feel safe.

with the peace i thought to be impossible...

i'm free. i'm free. i'm free, indeed.

i guess now
i could say that little girl was me.
the little girl
i never wanted to be
the one i wish
i never had to admit,
but i'm here.
giving to God
what i now know i can't bear.
embracing what's good,
so i can know i'm free.
don't get it wrong.
who the Son has set free
is free indeed.

that's me.

now this is my love letter,
lest i lose sight of myself
and someone tries to paint me blue.
this is my truth.

as i look back,
i see myself
blind and lost
taking my God for granted.
couldn't see, so i thought.
i had thoughts, things, people
telling me,
you are your own person,
and you are the master
of your own destiny.
i couldn't see so i heard.
i believed.
i believed
i... even i,
had the strength
to rebuild myself.
i had been deceived.
i had been defeated.
let down,
i made room for truth.
i apologized,
and put even myself behind.
repentance.
and as a mother comforts her child,
so does Yeshua comfort me.
now, there is no me
without He
who teaches the way.
He is
the Way,
the Truth
and the Life;
He gives Himself to me.
He gave Himself _for_ me.
now, i am so at peace.
not at the peace
the world had given me,
but the peace
that comes with pure satisfaction
surpassing all understanding.
He is
the Prince of Peace.
the One who justifies.
searching the reins and hearts,
He knows all and he sees all.
He that has given His all.
He that Has made me whole.
Truth.
it was not me who chose Him,
but He who chose me.
and forever shall i stay
at His feet.

rain down on me
oh, Holy Spirit.

You know i'm in need,
and You are the epitome.
my life,
ever changing.
Your grace,
Your love,
Your provision,
Your protection,
Your character
unchanging.
what joy it is
to be loved the right way.
the way i should be loved.
the way i am meant to be loved.
i open my heart
to receive,
but it's hard to believe.
thank You, Father,
for not getting tired of me.

thank You for loving me.

stand for something
or fall for anything.

that's true ain't it?
God is holding me afloat,
but as i fight,
i fight to get my mouth open.
i fight to speak.
i fight to stand.
i fight to not only be true
to my heavenly Father,
but i fight
to be faithful as His daughter.

even then,
the one with edge comes around
and i feel him near me,
telling me to tip over on his side.
it's been some time now
since he's been sending
unsolicited pictures from my memory.
that man i met...
the way he spoke to me...
i can tell
he thinks he's got some say about this
as though he's the Judge or the jury
because he keeps trying me,
mentioning that anger
i may have built up inside...
that choice i have to make.
the pressure.

good thing
my Father has enlarged my steps
so my feet don't slip...
no edge can ever cause me to dip.

hi!
well, as you know
my name is monique
and i'd like to speak.
that rhymed... heh.
it's my biggest weakness,
speaking, yet still a gift.
and now i can't help but see you glaring at me
as i begin to reach my peak.

it's a little early to be that high, no?

anyway,
that means you hear me.
are you listening?
of course.
i can't help but notice you tuning in.
i can't even think to grin.
wondering what else there is to say
when thoughts flash before my eyes.
those thoughts that double back
honestly, i may as well be on crack
it's euphoric.
thoughts that blur out right in front of my
face.
so, what's the case?

Lord,
You tell me you love hearing these words,
for sweet is thy voice...
mine?
i've personally painted the words for You...
for being so kind,
but i can't see why You'd see *me* as sublime.
open my eyes, Father.
and let me see things through Your eyes.
it's a struggle,
yet i get by.
all i know is i believe You.
okay, that's all i've got to say for now,
oh, and thanks for keeping me around.

hello,

my soul has been given a gift so deep,
i can finally feel the entirety of love.
{as far as i can handle, of course}
love and the pain
that comes along,
and yet have I not run away.

what it is to truly have a heart
soft enough to withstand love.
at times, overwhelming,
but never will I miss
my hardened heart of stone.

i'm finally here.
a cup emptied to be filled.
suffering long,
but I can finally withstand!
not by my strength,
but by His,
because He is.
He is.
He is.
He is
the Great I Am.
He is everything my heart needs.
He is everything I need to survive.

I want Him in my life.

as i stand,
i stand on top of a hill.
i've got a candle in my hand...
it's still lit.
i see darkness
way in the valley.
and the Light i behold sheds bright
on their nakedness.
i hear loud cries.
cries similar to a woman
giving birth to her dead child.
i hear discord and teeth gnashing.
but i also see hope looking up.
not to me,
but to the Light.
they see the way,
and as a good, good Father
would comfort His children,
there He goes
with His still, small voice, saying

come to Me...

sometimes,
i remember myself as the woman
who became in love with a man
who did not know how to love her back.
i remember myself as one
who sought to comfort those in pain,
rather than care for my own.
a tough lesson i had to learn...
i can only love them as far as i love myself.
seeking to create a habit
of acknowledging my heart,
i see pain and stress
trying to fight its way through.

feel, monique,
but don't get stuck.
wondering why my
my toughest habit to break,
is my disbelief of deserving love.
Lord, i believe;
help my unbelief.
i struggle to treat my body right.
between fasting
and inflicting starvation
rooted in self-hate,
i can't tell what i'm doing.
i work
and You give me,
Your beloved, sleep
and i struggle to receive.

not for long...

right now,

i wish i had more air to breathe.
i can't even see.
all pressure applied,
currently being blinded
by the steam.
i actually wish i could scream,
but i've given my air away.
got enough air to be frozen
for a moment,
that way i can just stay.
and rest.
i need air to breathe.
i wish i had more air to breathe.
i need to catch my breath...
better yet,
the Breath catches me.
even so my feet don't slip.
He catches me.

it feels like a new era.
surrounded by unfamiliarities,
i find peace in my Foundation.
i'm guided away from my past
towards new habits.
it's my Father who gets me.
my pain is no longer lonely.
it's my Father who holds me.
and i get it,
i'm not the only one.
it's you, too.
it's us...
just let me think
on my own for once.

dear human,

i forgive you.
i haven't written in so long,
but i thought
i'd write you a letter.
a letter of peace.
a letter of forgiveness...
hoping, maybe, this
will make things better.

i don't need an apology.
not from you.
despite what went down,
my only desire
is for you to hear me out.
would you want to do this for me?
because our memories
are in need of light.
and i want you here.
i want you here with me.

i want you here with me
so we can both breathe.

love,
monique

when I look him in his eyes,
it's as though time slows down...
and I like it,
yet it is just so unfamiliar to me.
so unfamiliar
that I break contact
after 7... gentle... seconds...

at most.

my heart gasps
because little me
had not known a love this deep
between the simple
and delicate
contact of the eyes.

i am pierced to a point of openness.
love is where I belong.

pain resides in me
and i cannot escape.
she sees me
as the broken girl i once was.
why can't i be seen as better?
why can't i be seen as whole?
is it so hard to imagine?
is it so hard to believe??
she sees me
as the broken girl i once was
and for a moment,
i feel like i can't move.
why can't i be seen as better?
i hate my life in this world,
i do.

i'm not depressed, no.

i just hate the way i'm so pressed
with faithless concern.
no. i just wish i could leave.
yet my Purpose says to wait.
although this world is not my home,
i have a woman to be while i'm here.
but can't you see?
i just want to be loved the right way.
they make it seem impossible,
making me wonder
if they can even say i'm so lovable.

picture this.

we sit in the fields
relating to the sprouts
in which arise out of their discomfort.
breaking, forming, blooming
into new openness
towards the Son.
we've lived in darkness,
yet Light lives...
and we are able to embrace
what it is to be loved.
yes, it hurts,
but peace comes.
i see that now.

Love is incredible.

it's like,
as you walk this journey with Christ,
your feet enters areas
in which love is exposed.
you are brought to breathe deeply
as this road
continues to make His name known.

the sweet melodies of His voice
teach you
about what love truly means.

His love is refreshing
as sight is for the blind.
it's purifying. it's divine.

so as you look into each other's eyes,
time will begin to slow down
and every good moment between you two
is highlighted in the sand.
you'd want nothing else to do,
but hold each other's hands
and walk this path,
as you become one.

and when you get under each other's skin,
you will remember how you have chosen
to grow in love.

in Love,
time stops
and the rising oceans
become gentle as a dove.

Spirit filled,
yet overflowing
in your cup
amongst those
who have no idea they'd desire
this same love.

this medicinal,
yet invisible aspect in your life
breaks chains
where your driest pains reside
in this land of yours.

yes,
His love is both patient
and kind.

Love smiles at you with hope...
even when you fall short.
no records of your wrongs,
so no more singing sad songs.
this Love
is right where you belong.

so cheers
to this everlasting beginning

because God's love
is very much unfailing.

breathe deeply
and recognize beauty.

can't you see?
God has made me this way.
not to define me
but to emphasize me.

i bleed passion,
and when i've been torn down
i rise
every. single. time.
i was made in the image of God.
my strength pure
and my skin jasper.
my kindness towards those who hate me
is not my weakness.

i am not my attributes to you
i'm not what i do.
you can look at the view,
but i'm not what you see.
i am not what's been done to me,
so quit trying to keep me in a box, please?

don't call me chocolate,
i'm not a snack.
don't call me sexy
because my name is monique.

honor me for who i am,
not how good i look in this red lipstick.
stop sexualizing me.
i am not just some delicacy
made for the pleasures of man
i am powerful
with God as my strength.

i am not the color you see,
but this color is apart of me.
my brown is not ugly,
it's deeper.
it's golden.
so keep folding
every time i find a new reason
to rise like the phoenix you are so afraid of.
or,
you can grow with me
and you can love me like the queen i am.
love me like Christ loves me.
love me like i love me.
love me because i'm lovable,
not because you see me as difficult.

[PAGE75]

He touched my heart to the point
where it meant something deeper
than i can ever imagine.
the calmness piecing joy
to what's normally meant
to wreak havoc

i can breathe

where the sun shines
and the winds blow...
as i look at you,
i see more than promises and rainbows.

it's love outside of time.
plus, it's just you and i.

-- it's freedom

i write
to bring back the timelessness
in which my peace reminds my heart
to smell the daisies
clothed in immense gratefulness.

dressed with care and worrilessness
with trust towards our Creator.

with just one stare,
i'm reminded to be still,
and know...

all while making it plain
i write in love

NOT THAT IT MATTERS,

...but i hope you see peace
when you look me in my eyes.

i hope you get choosy
when you speak,
hoping it'll bless me
out of your immense care for me.

i hope our good-bye's
are never reasons to cry...

because,
though you may be missing from me,
our hearts have been blessed for eternity.

therefore, it matters.

so please don't listen
to the chatters of my flesh,
for my soul yearns for truth instead.

can't keep getting my hopes up

in the wrong thing.
i'll just end up pleading
for my life to be scarce
once again.

afraid of the pain i might further face,
yet maybe this time
i could rise above the fence.

i prove,
yet i am not believed.
or maybe my desire to prove
is my own unbelief.

for if you believe,
then maybe i can finally
believe, too.
with you.

but i can't wait anymore
for you to value me,
if my God values me already.

regardless,
it's my turn now.

The Last of my beginning.

here's to letting go of the former things.

discomfort.

i found out discomfort is where my comfort lies.
twisted.
discomfort is where i let misunderstanding
take advantage of my innocence.

i breathe and i worry
everything will fall apart.
how can i expect things to be right with anyone,
if i'm not right with me?

i convince myself i can't breathe
because for a moment there
i think it's the only way
i can get away with being... me.
without anyone else knowing.

subtle silence.
no highlighting.
the scream without screaming.

mr. payne is always knocking on my door.
he's my friend, i think.
but i just don't trust him.
so i breathe in and breathe out
until his existence is gone,
but for a moment.
endurance is my best friend.
she hurts the most,
but there's always a reward right at the end.

it only takes one moment to suffer long.
it only takes one moment to suffer long.
multiple moments, maybe, where i'm tempted to sing
this extremely sad song.

uplift me.
that way my lungs have room to breathe.
that way i can stick to this peace
rather than my urge to worry.

comfort.

i can see comfort sometimes.
we play in the fields
as though not an ounce of heaviness exists.

freedom in air.
the worry leaves.
i'm steady.

comfort feels like a tempurpedic,
straight for my heart and my soul.
i couldn't ask for a better gift.
i'm waiting.

i'm waiting for more
because i hate sitting here feeling so sick
that i can't even sleep in my Comforter's arms.

as alarming as it is,
i see possibility where i hurt most.
the areas where touches make me cringe,
and my heart tolerates inconsistency.
more stiff than a woman traumatized.
oh, right, that's me.

comfort comes.
and comfort can indeed be permanent.
patience is my friend,
she tells me this comfort is imminent
and i believe her.

distrust.

nothing makes sense here
and neither does truth abide here.
just so you know...
1+3 never equals 4 here.

only lies prosper here.
lies and delusion.
they thrive here.

in my distrust, i freeze.
can't move because what will you do?
hate me or violate me?
exploit me or kill me?

take from me??

everyone has taken from me.
so much that i've
given my emptiness away to anyone willing to
take.
beautiful facade.
my vase looks pretty enough to create the
end of me
as i give my last to someone who throws glass
for the sake of destruction.

their warmth, my fire.
therefore, i struggle to trust now that i'm in
the downside up where my ashes are built to
beauty and strength.

renewed, yet the questions still pose them-
selves.

is this a test?

feelings.

i hurt so much,
i wonder when it'll end
almost every day.

joy stands in front of me
and i struggle to merely shake her hand.
why?

am i afraid something bad is going to happen?
do i not believe i deserve it?
where's my trust?

i can't think clearly
my pain is cloudy

i just need to see

why?

there's a touch.
sensations in which bring about my
anxiousness.
my anticipation.
my vulnerabilities,
i almost cant bear this weakness.
dewey repetitions,
and the constant thought of:

why am i here?

holes.

i can't keep digging myself
in holes i know i cannot breathe in.
i can't keep doing this.
the blood on my hands,
giving me thoughts
of uncertainty towards my recompense.
i didn't mean to.
i didn't mean to hurt you.
i didn't mean to hurt you,
i didn't.

i disregarded you
and forced the thought of us
to be undeserving.
you can't love me the way you say you do.

i lack belief.
it even hurts me to hear you speak.
i can't trust you.
i'm sorry.
i need help
if i'm going to choose better.
better for us.
better.
better for everyone.
i can't trust myself, either, though.
or what i say.

and if my heart condemn me,
then my confidence in Christ is ....
it's missing.
i didn't mean for this to happen.
i didn't.

a process.

so i relearn myself
and i'm molded,
yet my pieces get broken
to bring forth my wholeness.

my uneasiness
brought by this centrifuge
is excused.

i can't wait to be free!
but i'm free now.
temporarily bound
in this painful silence
yea, i'm frowning.
my agony is loud,
and my joy is imminent.

i'm eager to see where my story ends.
so i breathe deeply
and remember today.

i relearn myself
and i'm molded,
yet my pieces get broken
to bring forth my wholeness.

and then...
i rejoice.

i'm home.

it started with a desire
to be where peace is.
where love burns so deep,
its fire is invincible against the punches.
it started with a hate
for my life in this world.
my inclination is purely innate.
it started when i was six.
i yearned for a place
better than the house i lived in.
"spoiled brat,"
if anyone knew i wanted more
they'd call me selfish.
it started with a hope.
a hope i didn't even know i had.

it started with knowing
this world is not my home.

october 30, 2020
berrien springs, michigan

3:47am

this morning,
to my surprise,
i heavily imagined my suicide.
not that i truly want to die,
rather, i wanted to see how it felt
to genuinely give up on this life...
without the commitment.
i was pretty upset.
and i don't want to sound depressing,
so i hope you can handle it
when i tell you the secrets that go deepest.

because in this specially curated heat,
i saw myself give in to what seemed impending.
is this... is this deceit?
it's as though i'm looking at another person
while i sit in this sorrow-filled burden.
and before i watch her leave,
i cry out my apologies to those i have loved most...
and to those who love me.
my pain overflowed,
a purge began and i was being emptied --

something broke in me,
then disappearance embedded on her
like cotton candy.

and i saw my life replay once more:

one.

truth be told,
my heart's been broken from young.
i hated my life in this world,
took six years to see my life as dumb.
sweet girl, wishing to go home...
and i couldn't.
because, where was it?

and there i was,
lost in my ignorance.

<u>two.</u>

i was lost for years.
i was easily brought to tears.
i was emptied.
all i had left
were my hate and my fears.
fantasized about my death,
yet still chose to believe

maybe one day
i could breathe.

three.

i'm not done,
but i'm free.
free from the bondage
y'all didn't know was in me.
i can breathe.
i can finally hear myself speak
even in the midst of all my enemies.

<u>four.</u>

generational curses broken,
now there's room to grow more.
generational cycles being shaken,
i'm being groomed from my very core.
and it's hard,
but i see now
God cares enough to never leave me
where i've been before.

<u>five.</u>

i rest here with grace,
where i'm seated outside of time.
i'm unworthy
of receiving this type of paradise.
created for love,
i take the dive...
again and again,

<u>six.</u>

i found comfort in my pain,
but now...
i dont want to merely exist as i did,
i want to live.
i want to conquer.
i want to uplift.

<u>seven.</u>

"yet not my will,
but Yours be done,
on earth as it is in heaven."

the Ending.

this morning,

i died to myself.
and in my constant renewal,
i live

again and again.

yet not i,
but Christ lives in me;
and the life i now live in the flesh
i live by faith in the Son of God,
who loved me and gave Himself for me.

"know this, that every story has an ending
where every question has an answer.
Jesus, being that very answer,
is our boast for we are made whole through him.

rejoice,
for we are overcomers
by the Messiah who overcame!"

- Ty

*"Teacher,
which is the great commandment in the law?"*

*Jesus said to him, "You shall love the Lord your God
with all your heart, with all your soul,
and with all your mind. This is the first
and great commandment. And the second is like it:
You shall love your neighbor as yourself."*

now that you've reached the end of my book,

you will realize the focus of my writing shifted
as the story progressed...

that's because as i kept growing, and writing,
i became deeply in love with who God is.

and with the fact that *He is love...*

it amazes me how loving He is, actually.
and how gentle He is, even with His rebuke.

so my book is not merely about a man
i chose to love.. neither is it merely about me
seeing a reason to love myself, or others.
it's also about what God did in the midst of those
things... in the midst of both my joy and my pain,
to lead me back to my true first love, which is Him.
it's about how He's been Faithful
to love me in my ugliness.

not many will believe this, but i do.
and i can honestly say, God. is. alive.
and He is more of a personal God
than we've ever been taught.
so much, He'll even help you pick out an outfit
for the day.
so much that He'll be your best friend as you brush
your teeth and vent your own life
away into His hands.

He smiles....

any who, i could talk about Christ all day,
so let me leave it on this note:

in love, we suffer at times,
but it will always be worth it.

would i choose to go through it all again?
no. but that's not a requirement. LOL.

it gets better
because _we_ get better

- Lyttle Monique

<u>references!! via the KJV bible!</u>

[Prelude]
- God is love: 1 John 4:16; 1 John 4:8
- Christ of God: Luke 9:20

[Preface]
- All things w. Christ: Philippeans 4:13

[#5]
- Delight in the Lord: Psalms 37:4

[#7]
- Heart is deceitful: Jeremiah 17:9-10
- God's grace sufficient: 2 Corinthians 12:9
- God is love: 1 John 4:16; 1 John 4:8;
1 Corinthians 13:4-8; Galatians 5:22-23
- Those who labor: Matthew 11:28
- Lay down his life: John 15:13-15
- Peace: Philippeans 4:6

[#8]
- Spirit of power: 2 Timothy 1:7

[#10]
- God's plans: Jeremiah 29:11

[#11]
- Take this cup: Matthew 26:39; Luke 22:42

[#12]
- For those who love God: Romans 8:28

<u>references!! via the KJV bible!</u>

[#20]
- Speak Lord: 1 Samuel 3:10

[#25]
- Step on their necks: Joshua 10:24-25

[#33]
- Wind blows: John 3:8

[#34]
- Free indeed: John 8:36

[#37]
- Enlarged my steps: Psalm 18:36; 2 Samuel 22:37

[#38]
- For sweet is thy voice: Song of Solomon 2:14

[#40]
- Come to me: Matthew 11:28

[#41]
- Help my unbelief: Mark 9:24
- Give me sleep: Psalm 127:2

[holes]
- if my heart condemn me: 1 John 3:21

[seven]
- Luke 22:42; Matthew 6:10; Galatians 2:20

[law of love]
- Matthew 22:36-40

thank you,
for believing in me.

CPSIA information can be obtained
at www.ICGtesting.com
Printed in the USA
BVHW030841240621
610369BV00006B/131